If only you knew how much I smell you

True portraits of dogs

Photographs by Valerie Shaff

Text by Roy Blount Jr.

Bulfinch Press

AOL Time Warner Book Group

Boston • New York • London

These photographs are dedicated with gratitude to all the animals,
for what they teach us gracefully about living and loving
— V.S.

For Thelma, Filona, Stella, and Spot
— R.B.

Introduction

Roy Blount Jr.

Maybe it's rude, but I will often say hi to a dog in the street without even glancing at the person walking the dog. The response is usually a look from the dog that says, "I'm with him [or her]," but that's cool.

Every now and then I'll make corner-of-the-eye contact with a dog tied to a parking meter outside a grocery, and the dog will say, "Do you know her [or him]? I guess you don't, but . . . (Sigh.) Will she [or he] ever come out?"

"Sure, hang in there," I say.

"Easy for you to say," says the dog.

When I was in my teens, my younger sister, Susan, who loves dogs (Hi there, Stella), got a dog whistle from somewhere. The kind that only dogs are supposed to hear. Chipper, our dog at the time (and for many years), was lying on her back on the floor. Susan blew the whistle.

Nothing.

"Chipper. Did you hear that?"

Chipper, a black-and-white blend of various terriers, opened one eye. It was hard to tell, upside down as she was, but she appeared to smile slightly before the eye closed again. Susan adjusted the whistle, to lower its pitch, and blew it again.

Chipper's smile was gone now. Her features were immobile, except for a slight tremor in her upper lip where it hung slightly away from her mouth as a dog's upper lip will do when she is asleep on her back.

"That time *I* heard it," I said.

Chipper opened one eye and gave me a look.

"Don't go there," that look said.

Many years later, my then-wife and I had a dog named Peggy, a sweet, dignified cross between some kind of bulldog and something longer-legged, who got pregnant when she was just about a year old. Worried that she was too young to know what to do, we sat up late with her as she delivered seven healthy bullish pups on the couch. That's where she wanted to have them. We had put a sheet under her. She licked them all clean, got them all nestled against her side, seemed to be bushed but on top of the situation. Joan told her good night and went to bed, but I wasn't quite satisfied. "I'm impressed," I told Peggy. She nodded pleasantly, narrowed her eyes as if about to go to sleep, and then had puppy number eight. As she finished tidying up that last one and gave me a little grin, just between the two of us, in the middle of the night, she was saying — well, who knows, maybe she was saying, "Maybe if you'll leave, they'll stop coming." But I think she was saying, "Yep. Ain't I a bitch?"

I read somewhere that Toulouse-Lautrec became such great friends with an anteater in the Paris zoo that the anteater would actually jump up and down in anticipation when Lautrec approached. Maybe Lautrec just assumed it was anticipation. It may have been agitation. I've never been around anteaters enough to say how well a French painter might read them.

We *know* what it means when a dog, on seeing us, jumps up and down. That is, we know what it means to *us:* it means that as long as that dog is alive and can find us, we will never be alone in the world.

How well do we know what it means to the dog?

When I was growing up, we would talk not only to, but also for, our dogs, and to each other through our dogs. "Chipper says, 'Bubba, you were gone so *long* this time,' " my mother might say for Chipper, who would then look embarrassed. Our dogs sometimes appeared to be muttering to themselves. But they would jump up and down when they saw us coming.

People can talk to dogs and also stroke them manually. Dogs want to respond —
but they can't talk, they don't have hands, and people generally don't like being
licked, humped, or sniffed much.

There are coarse, unsubtle dogs:

> Stop smellin' so vague.
> I'll bite yer damn laig.

And there are arch, overbred dogs:

> "Hi there," couple of pats.
> "Nice dog, do you bite?"
> Pat 'n' chatter: that's
> What people call *polite*.
>
> Umm . . . excuse me? People!
> All hands and blather.
> Anyone else — a *sheep*'ll
> Sense a dog would rather —
>
> I don't know, I've never
> Worked with sheep, of course,
> But sheep, cows, whatever —
> Can you imagine a *horse*
>
> Groping and mouthing clichés?
> And horses — please — aren't *smart*,

But a horse at least neighs
Or whatever from the heart,

And has, when sniffed, the courtesy
To stop and smell the roses.
People! We'd all prefer to see
Them get in touch with their noses.

All dogs communicate by means other than words. Since with people, sniffing is at best a one-way street, dogs try to make themselves clear to us by dint of yips, arfs, whines, growls, and grumbles, also frisking, jumping, nestling, and pawing — and they give us looks. Until a photographer comes along who *is* a dog, and a good one, I don't think we will see the expressiveness of dogs' looks captured better than in

Valerie Shaff's
Photographs.

Oddly enough, she started with livestock. She strikes me as a person of high enthusiasm, but "one summer," she says, "I was depressed, I couldn't move — the only thing that got me out of it was to ride my bike to a pasture of cows or a pigsty. They make you laugh so much." She brought a camera. "People started wanting me to take pictures of their farm animals. Then they started asking me if I would photograph their dogs."

Now, jet-set dog owners commission her. "The Richard Avedon of dog photography," she was called by the *New York Observer*. I'd say she is more sympathetic to her subjects than that.

Dogs, for their part, don't necessarily respond to a photographer's needs. They have what you might call short session spans. "There was a little white dog, Pooker, who refused to sit up. I needed to put him on something too small to lie down on. I used a flowerpot. The only time I feel a dog has defeated me is if it's a little trauma-tized 'rescued' dog. It might be just fine if it's in somebody's arms, but otherwise. . . . You're not going to re-create this dog's character in an hour."

To get dogs to look, she sometimes makes high-pitched *eeeeeee* noises, or yips like a dog herself, or meows, or exclaims, *"Where's the squirrel?"* What many of the dogs in this book may be thinking is, *"What* in the . . . ?" But isn't that what dogs seem to be thinking a good deal of the time, in reaction to human behavior?

For instance, you know this is something that a dog will never understand:

"Who ever came up with the notion of 'Down, boy'? Where does that even come from in the human mind? We want to jump up on people! To show we like them!"

Valerie has an eye for dogs' eyes, I know that. I don't think I've ever seen such evocative eyes in photographs of dogs — I know I haven't in photographs of people. She catches dogs having fun by themselves, but most poignantly she catches dogs doing their best — while remaining their own dogs — to come to terms with peo-ple. When Valerie shoots a dog, you want to pet him or let him out or throw him a stick.

Or put words in his mouth. A tricky proposition. Let's face it, we don't know for sure what dogs are thinking. We don't know what people are thinking unless they tell us, and then they may be lying. Dogs don't lie. In fact I'd say they have a con-fessional streak, as I believe anyone who has come home a few seconds after a dog has hastily got down from the couch will agree.

But dogs can't talk. Dogs may wish that people couldn't either, so that the two species could run through the woods together on an equal footing. Since people can and do talk, however, I think it's pretty clear that dogs would like to be able, occasionally, to say something — if only, "All right! I take your point!"

A word, here, about the difference between dogs and cats. I like cats. I want to make that clear, because when I have compared dogs to cats in the past, I have been lumped in with Hitler and Mussolini. ("Hitler and Mussolini hated cats" is often the way an outraged cat person will *begin* a letter to a perceived cat denigrator.) I have related amicably to — in several cases lived fairly harmoniously with — a number of cats, and they to me. But I have never felt tempted to imagine what cats are thinking. The only thing I feel I can say with confidence about what does or does not go on in a cat's mind is that a cat is not interested in what is going on in mine, either.

In fact it is in some ways more relaxing to be around a cat than a dog, because a cat will just stare right back at a person until the cat goes to sleep or the person looks away. A dog won't. A dog will meet a person's gaze for a moment, go soft-eyed, blink, glance off, get self-conscious, conceivably wink. Show concern. Sigh.

Meaningfully. But meaning what, exactly?

It is an *issue* between dogs and people, that dogs can't talk and people can. Little wonder, then, that people are sorely tempted to speak for dogs.

My friends the Bettses used to have a dog named Cinnamon, who was always timid and who in her old age became deaf and blind. Once ten or twelve of us people were sprawled all over the Bettses' living room telling loud stories and laughing, when Cinnamon entered looking lonesome, walked slowly all the way through the middle of the room, without bumping into anyone, as it happened, and out the other door. We fell silent.

"Well," said Roland Betts, speaking for Cinnamon, "*nobody in here.*"

Later the Bettses got a hearty bulldog and named him Maxx. Once when they were visiting me, the neighborhood bully dogs came over, converged on Cinnamon, and threatened her. I almost never think a dog is bad, but these dogs would attack any dog or person who didn't stand up to them. Maxx came around the corner, walked unhurriedly up to the bad dogs until his head was within a few inches of both their throats (they were a head taller than he was), and looked at them. Didn't even growl. After a moment, you could *hear* the bad dogs saying, "Uh, we were just, uh, welcoming . . . Listen, we were just going home, and by the way, if you want *our* property, you can have it. We're not even dogs, really . . ."

In time Cinnamon passed away, and the Bettses got another bulldog, a little one named Mona. Maxx did not pretend to be overjoyed, but he did seem to take Mona under his wing, so to speak. She shared his bed, I know that. However, one evening I walked in on them in the Bettses kitchen, and I *swear* I caught Maxx whispering to Mona, "They love it when you pee on the rug." Mona never got housebroken and had to be given away. Maybe dogs do lie sometimes, to each other.

In my efforts to speak for the dogs in Valerie's photographs I found myself drawn into verse. *Doggerel* is a word that probably meant, originally (the first usage cited in the *Oxford English Dictionary* is by Chaucer in 1386), verse fit for a dog. Low, irregular verse. Since then, we have come a long way in our estimation of dogs.

Back in the early eighties (when Truman Capote regularly turned up on talk shows), Nora Ephron and I were going to write the book and lyrics, respectively, of a Broadway musical. We got as far as a plot and a few songs, one of which was to be sung by a character playing a New York dog named Alice.

Alice:

My sister lives on spacious grounds
And chases rabbits often.
My cousin is a coyote.

Whereas, me,
I lie around,
Watch TV,
Feel my muscles soften,
And growl at Truman Capote.
(Only dogs hear some of the sounds
That come from Truman Capote.)

No grass around but little smidgens,
Nothing around to chase but pigeons,
Or maybe an occasional plaster-of-Paris frog.
Oh, it's hard to be an ur . . . ban —
Nobody wants to pee on a curb, an'
Have their . . . poop . . .
Scooped.
Oh! It's hard to be an ur . . . ban
Dog!

I strain at my leash as I walk through the smog.
There's a law against chasing those people that jog.
I get a little weepy as I sig my sog:

It's hard . . . to be . . . an ur . . . ban . . .
Dog!

Do you know the recitation "Old Shep"? How might such a poem go if it were composed by a dog paying nostalgic tribute to a person rather than vice versa?

Let's say the poet is a dog who grew up in the bosom of an elderly couple, who have gone on to their reward. "Old Alice and Harold Simmons," by Brownie. If canine verse were humanesque, the first stanza might run along these lines:

> I came to them when they were old.
> Their wrinkled hands were kind.
> Right from the start I knew that I'd
> Be theirs, and they'd be mine.

The final stanza, along these:

> Whatever thing in life they had,
> With me they'd always share.
> If people have a heaven, then
> I know I'll see them there.

But these, after all, are iambic feet, ba-DUM, ba-DUM: the rhythm (with perhaps a hitch here and there) of *bipedal* getalong, a *person* walking. Wouldn't a dog's meter be different? Four beats to the measure? Dit-dit-dit-DAH would be too ominous, like the opening of Beethoven's Fifth. What's a canine tempo? Consider Stephen Foster's "Camptown Races." Racehorses running are earnest, driven, as in "Gwine to run all night, gwine to run all day." Running dogs (*pace* Mao Zedong) are frolicky, irregular, as in "I bet my money on a bobtail nag, somebody bet on the bay." We might isolate the basic canine meter in "gwine to run all" or "money on a": *Dah*-dit-dit-dit. So:

Old though-they-were
Pup though-I-was
Love entered-my
Fur through-their-paws.

No. Sounds like that jing-a-ling song about Christmas bells. Dogs' feet vary. Doglegs crook. Canine measure is somewhere between ordered and free.

It's not a good idea to write about one's human relationships, because the other person might read it, and exclaim, "He thinks *that* was our relationship?" But I was just thinking how much of this one relationship was organized around someone else's dog. Spot. My friends the Swans' Jack Russell terrier. My girlfriend and I would go up to the country, where the Swans are my neighbors down the road, and we would take Spot for the weekend. I hate to say this, but I think Spot was my favorite dog. I would walk into the Swans' house and he would come running and jump, *sproing*, right straight up into my arms. My girlfriend loved dogs, too, and particularly Spot. We were his stepparents. We'd take Spot for a walk and, Lord, he loved it. He'd spring through the air like an eland or something, a springbok. Spring and bark. The problem was, he wanted — needed, *intended* — to spring and bark twelve to fourteen hours a day, and if he'd had a Ph.D. in Communications he still would not have known the meaning of fear, or even prudence. And I don't have a fence. I took him outside and looked him in the eye and said, "Spot. Stay with me. Run around in the yard. But don't go over there where the bad dogs live. Okay? Stay. Okay?"

He gave me a pained, fond, deeply disappointed look. The sort of look that Uma Thurman (say) might give you if she cared for you, and wanted to think of you as a kindred spirit, and you were telling her that we *had* to spend, for *her* sake, a quiet evening at home. A look as if to say, "I hear you! But I'm hurt. With the bond you and I have, you still speak to me — me — as if you can tell me what's good for me? And it's *staying?*" The minute I turned around, Spot was gone, looking for action.

He wasn't going to pick a fight, he was like his friend Maxx in that regard, but he wasn't going to be intimidated either, and each of those mean dogs was four times his size. He could probably have backed either one of them down individually, but together they could have hurt him, the way I'd seen them hurt my son's dog Thelma, a venturesome beagle of spirit. You should have seen Spot and Maxx and Thelma chasing each other in circles. But when Thelma went to play with the mean dogs, they ripped her stomach open. There was no talking to the mean dogs. They would come into my yard and snarl at me. I like to feel I can talk to any dog, but these I had to chase away. I don't know what was wrong with those dogs. Their owners were very nice people. When I went to their house to complain about their hurting Thelma, the dogs stopped romping with the young children who loved them and bounded effusively up to me as if to say, "Oh! You're the nice man from across the road!" Dogs *do* lie.

Even Spot. Because he gave me every indication (well, he sat down) that he would stay. He was going to come *back*, of course. But he wasn't about to *stay*. He was a dog. Too much dog. I had to run him down — which was not easy — and yell at him and keep him tied up, except when we were indoors (at night he would wriggle way down under the covers and sleep between my feet), or he was out springing and barking through the woods. Spot was a full-time occupation. He would stand in the front seat of the car, with his feet on the dash, and stare intently ahead as if he were navigating. I'd say to him, "It's okay, Spot, I know where we're going," and he'd give me this look like, "I'll be the judge of that" — but there would be a little smile playing around the edges of his intensity. Spot is the only dog I've known who could keep an almost completely straight face while giving you a partly tongue-in-cheek look.

Before Spot, the Swans had Trim. To begin with, Trim was big and simple — a cross between a black Lab and several larger things — and then he got hit in the head by a car. It left him not quite right. He *always* had a pinecone in his mouth. But good-hearted? Outside in a hutch the Swans had a rabbit, named Bun. They worried that Bun would get out and Trim, being a dog, would hurt him. One afternoon they heard a scratching and thumping at their screen door and they looked, and there were Trim's face and Bun's face, side by side, both of them wanting to get in the house.

The peaceable kingdom. The lion down with the lamb. People interfacing with, well, animals.

I can't be sure what Spot would say if he could read this. I haven't seen him in years. He exhausted the Swans and two subsequent families before finally getting a little older and settling down. But I could swear that dog understood every word I said.

"That's just an expression," people say. Well, what isn't?

Let's go.

No?

Why not?

Not *now?*

What's *now?*

No?

Let's go.

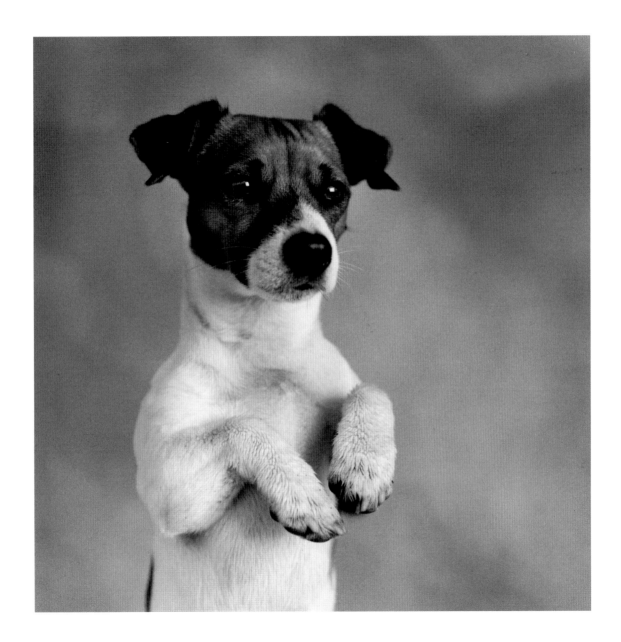

Good stick.

Got a good stick.

A real

    good

Stick.

Getting all the good

Out of this good

Stick

That's in

This

    good

Stick.

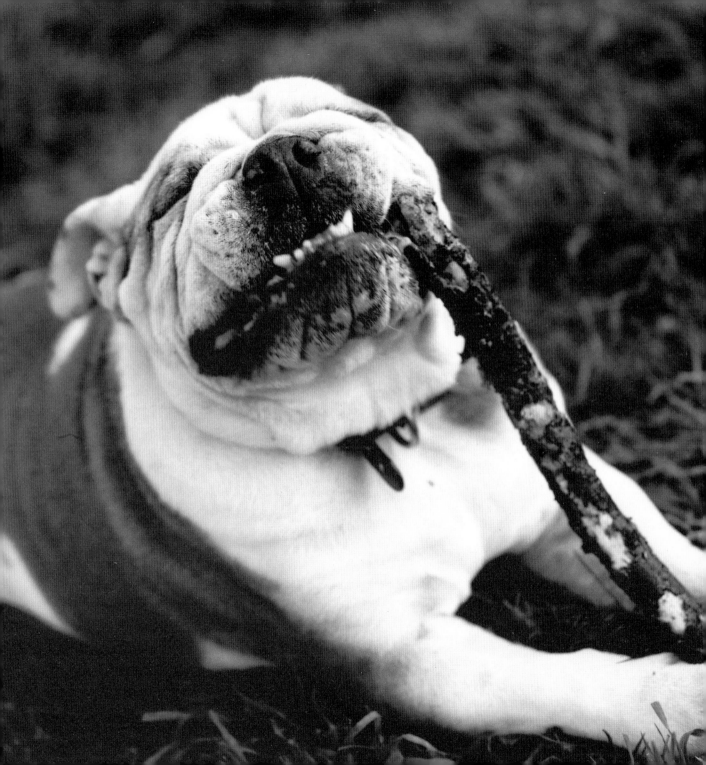

The bird, the bee
Know what to do,
But part of me
Still looks to you.

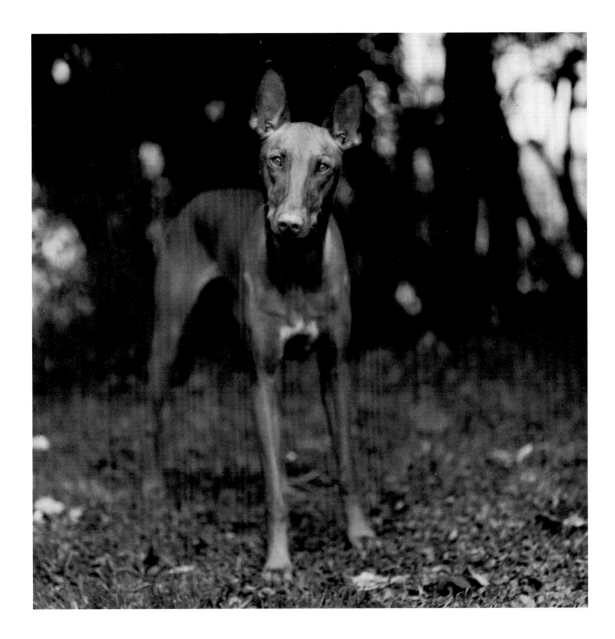

Fluffy, yes, we hear that a lot.
We *are* quite fluffy. And you are not.

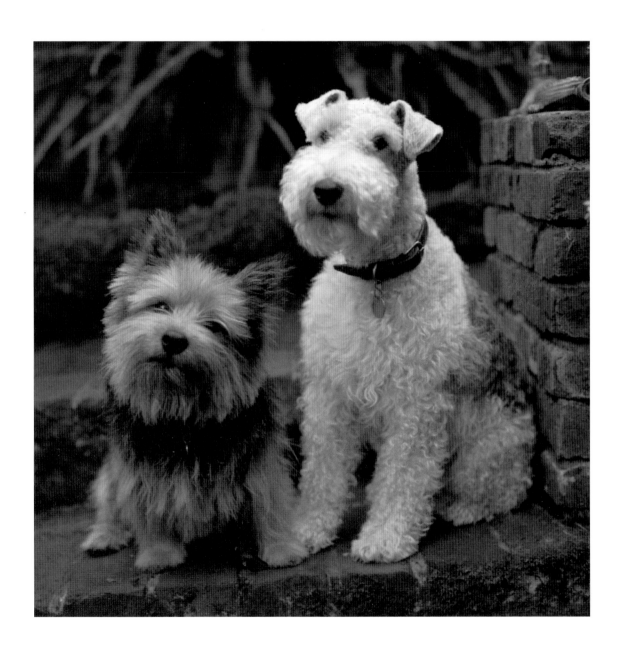

Interesting water.
Whatever might
Come by in this water,
I'm set to bite.

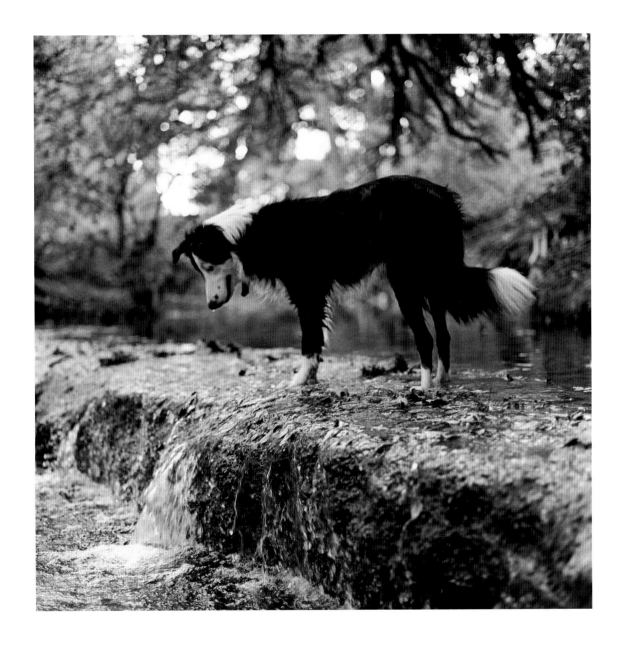

How I
Get high:
By going
Boing!

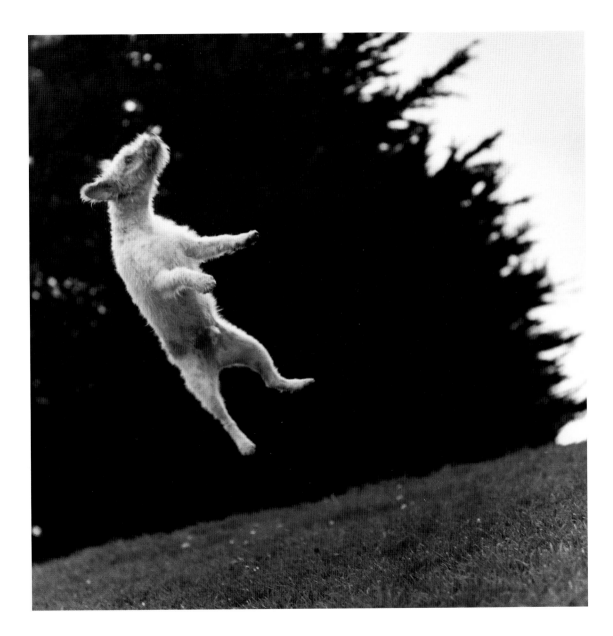

When? Now!
How? This way!
Here comes the sun,
I love to run —
A dog knows how
To seize the day.

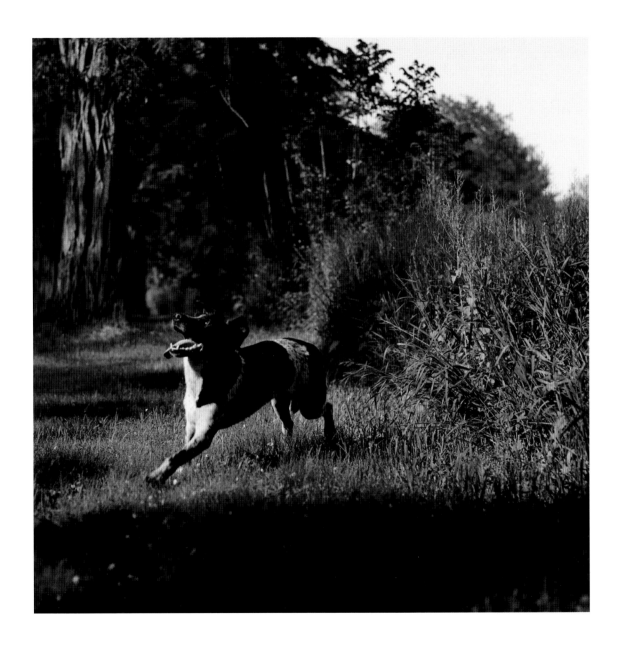

"Gone to college,"
Is what they said.
To my knowledge,
That means he's dead.

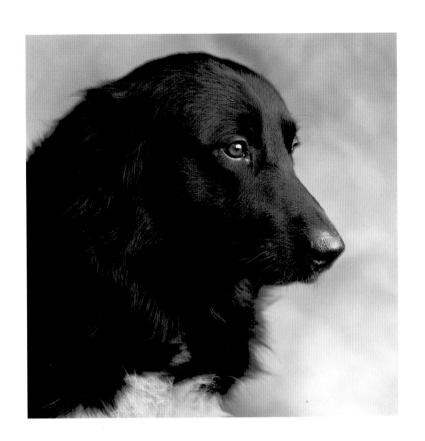

I have seen a great deal of the world.
People are pretty much the same.

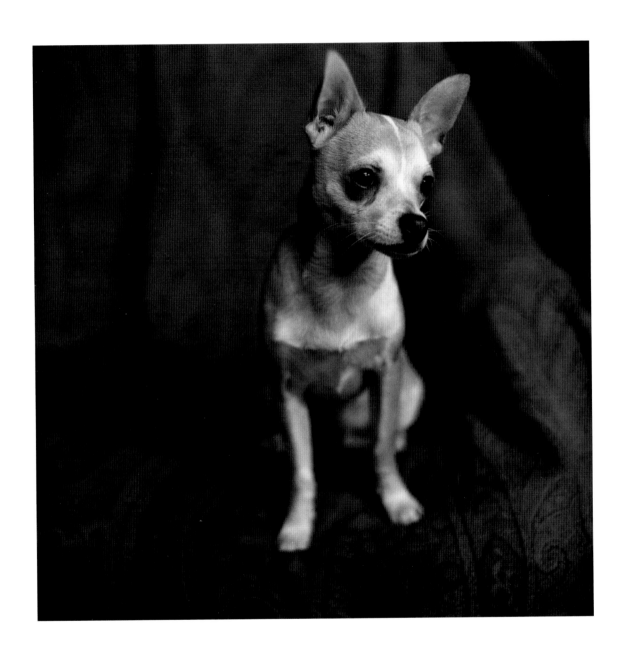

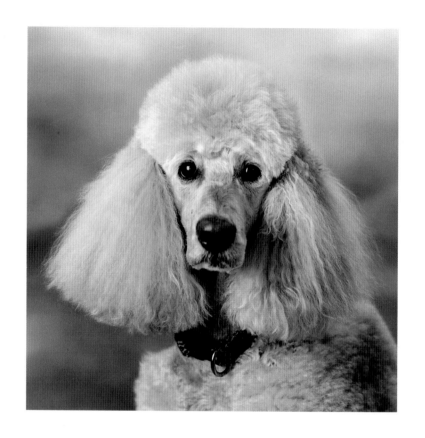

We have quite a lot in common,
Actually.
We're both not one drop mixed.

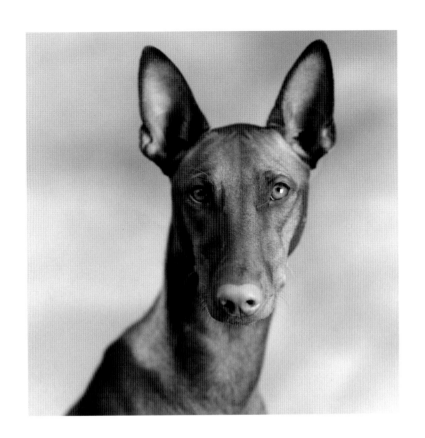

Ergo, not one drop common.

Sexually,

We've both been fixed.

Giving *you* such a look?

What are you, an open book?

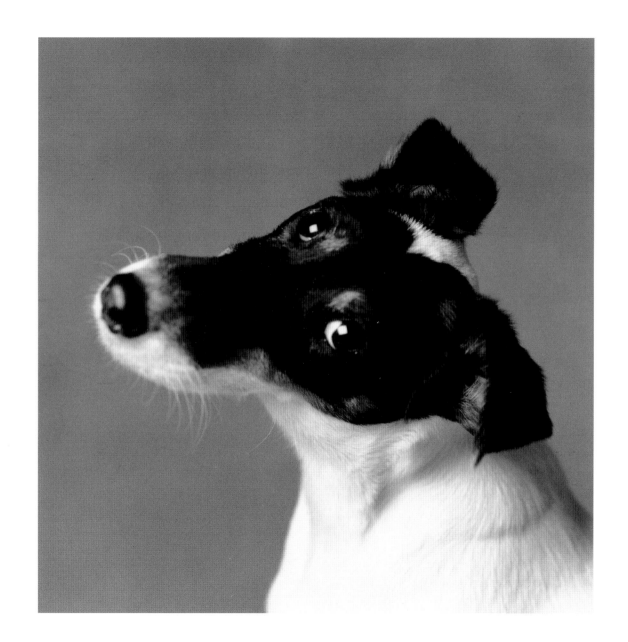

You're the boss, no doubt about that.
So, give me a reassuring pat.
Did you ever wonder, if you were as small
As me, would you dare to look up at all?

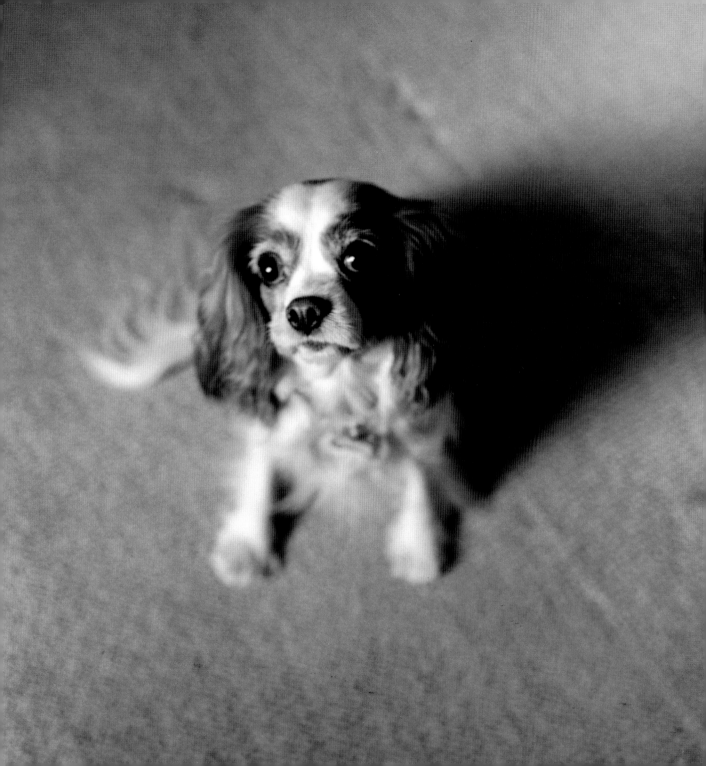

Yes,
A nice day. Yes,
A pretty spot. I'm
Eleven years old and I'm
Digesting a chicken
Bone. Yes,
I shouldn't eat chicken
Bones. I know.
I k n o w .

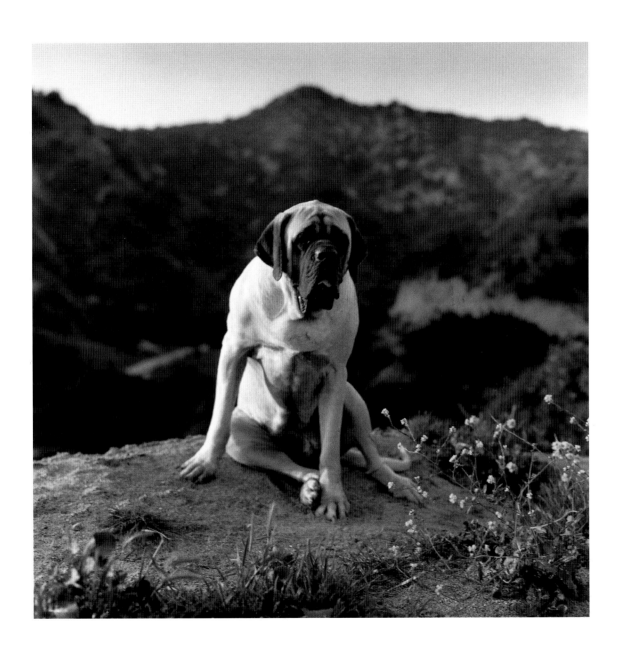

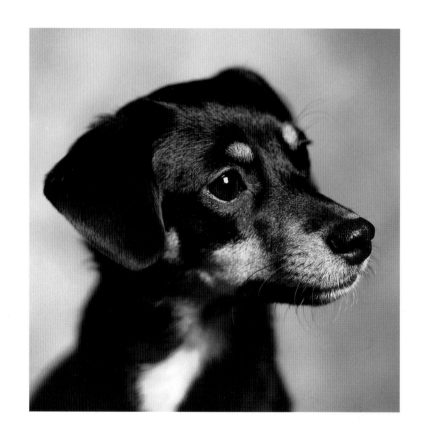

What they say, we do,

And we get fed

Kibble? Who cut that deal?

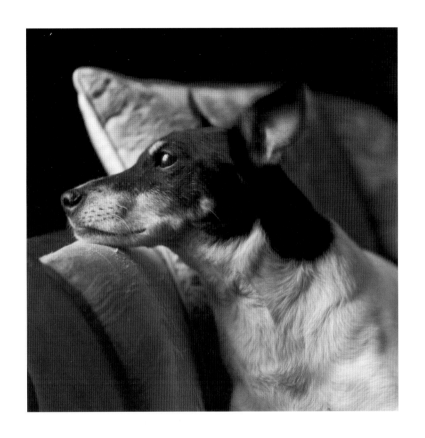

I asked that, too,

At your age, lad.

I hear you, but . . . I deal.

You look at me as if there were
Something I should register —
Some kind of issue, master-to-pet,
For you to know and me to get.
What? What? I'm pretty, smart,
Appealingly small, and yet my heart
(Courage- and also affection-wise),
As any fool can see in my eyes,
Is larger than yours, and purer, and yet

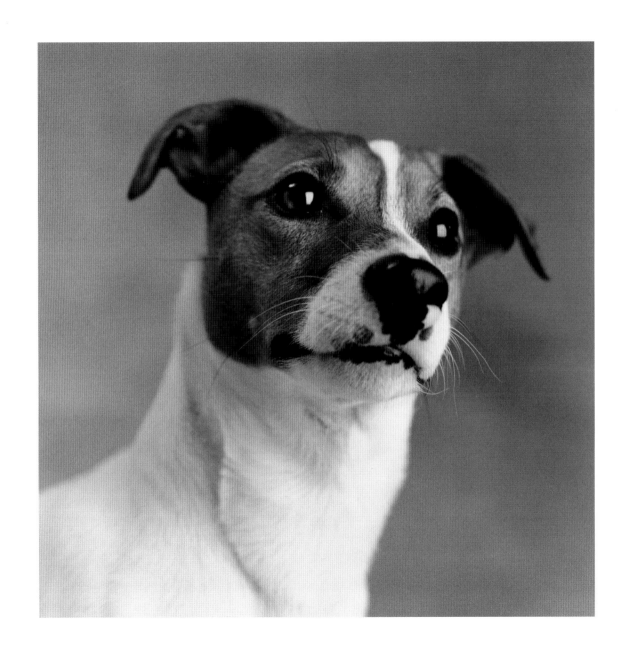

I don't make a point of it. So! Let's get
It on! You walk, I'll run and leap
For an hour or two and then I'll sleep
In your lap for a while and then let's eat!
Then do it all again! Life's sweet!

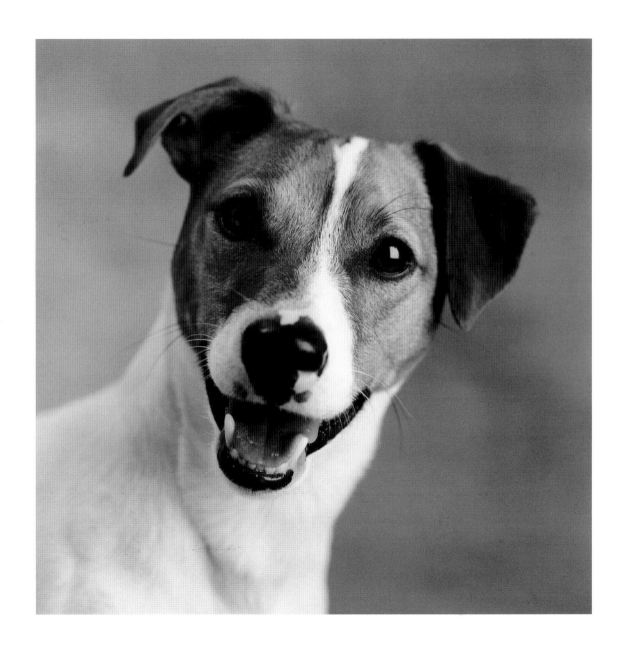

How can you be

So blindly smitten . . .

You have me,

And you pet that kitten?

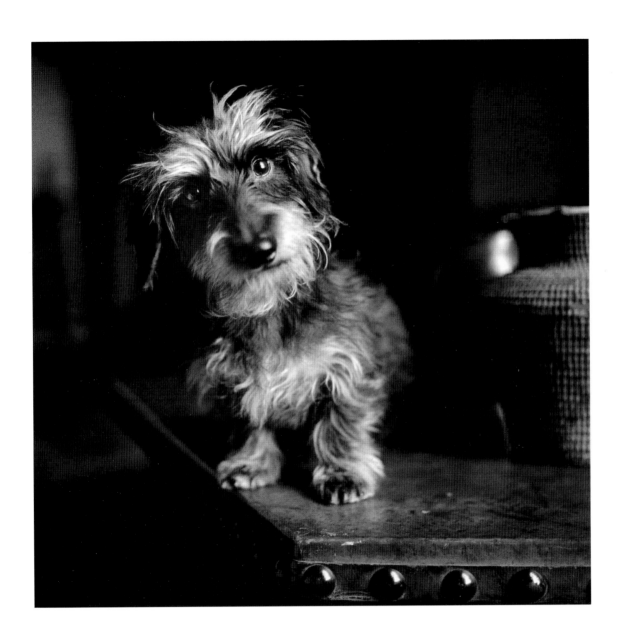

People fret
About "seeking their bliss."
It doesn't get
Any better than this.

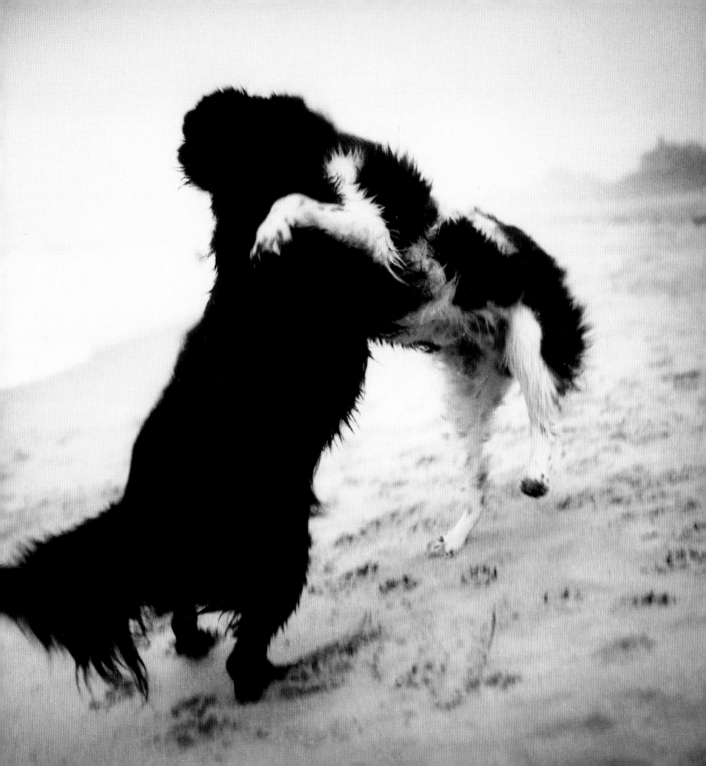

Though I am, as ever, yours,
Of this situation — outdoors
And the air clear as a bell
To anyone who can smell,
Whereas, to you, it's *misty* —
It would not be egotisti-
Cal of me to feel I'm master.

Can't you walk a little faster?

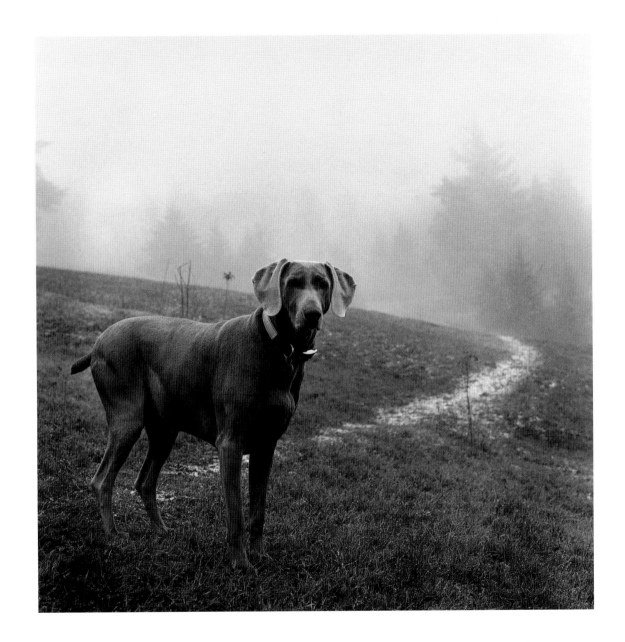

Oh, "beautiful, beautiful"! If I hear that again,
I think I'll go out of my mind.
Do you have any idea how long it has been
Since anyone sniffed my behind?

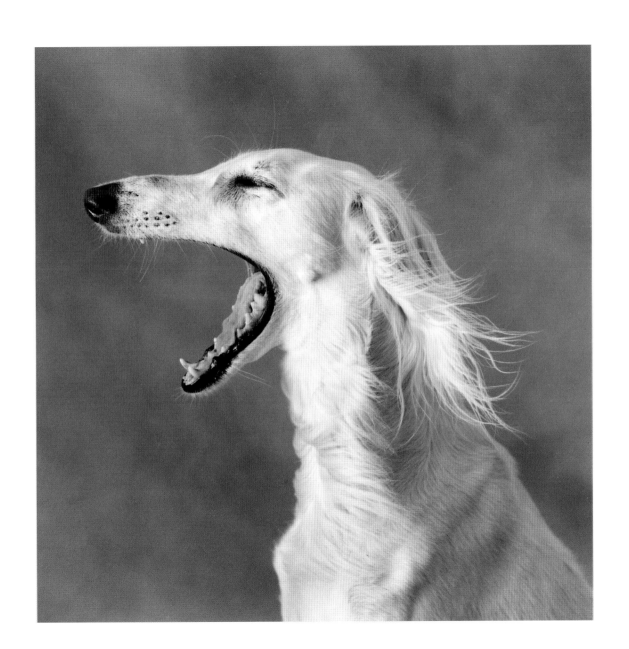

You can ask anybody,
You can look it up.
Nothing is as pretty
As a spotted pup.

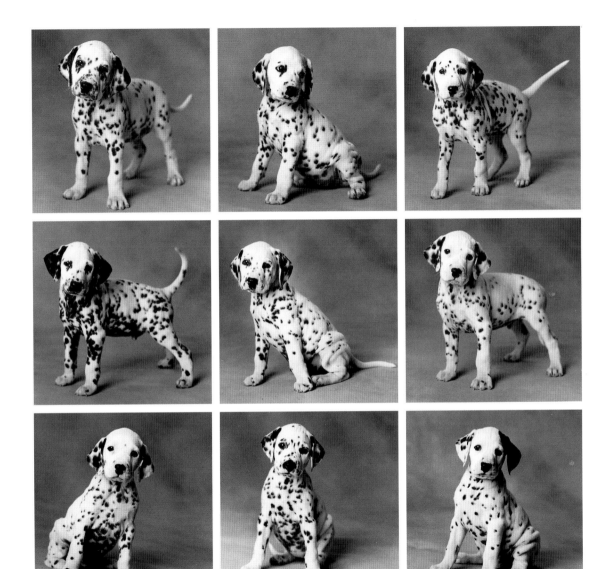

Oh, right, you're bad.
Try something, go ahead.
Just remember,
I'm your mama.

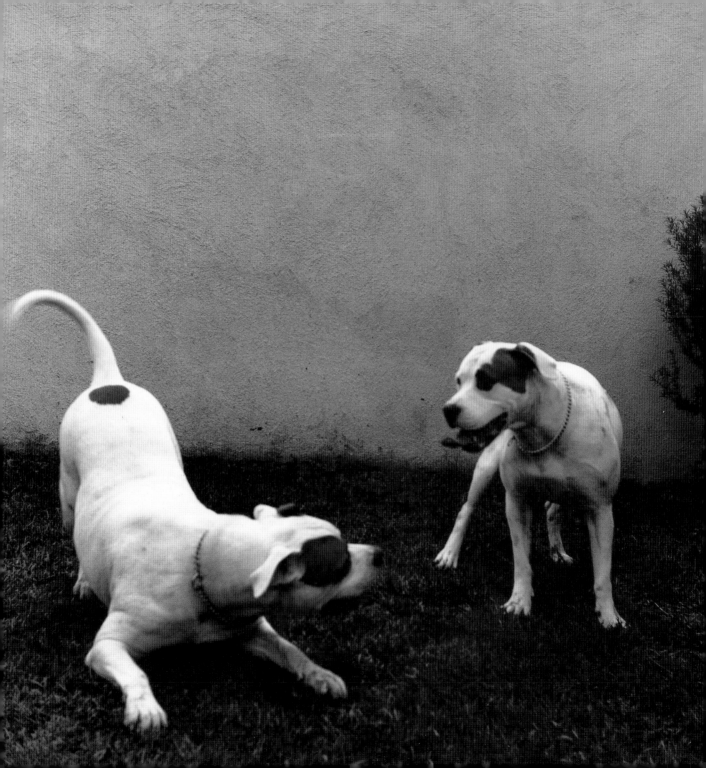

Feel a little itchy,
Got a little ache?
Don't get bitchy,

Shake,
Wriggle, and roll.

That's all it'll take —

Shake,
Wriggle, and roll —

To save your doggone soul.

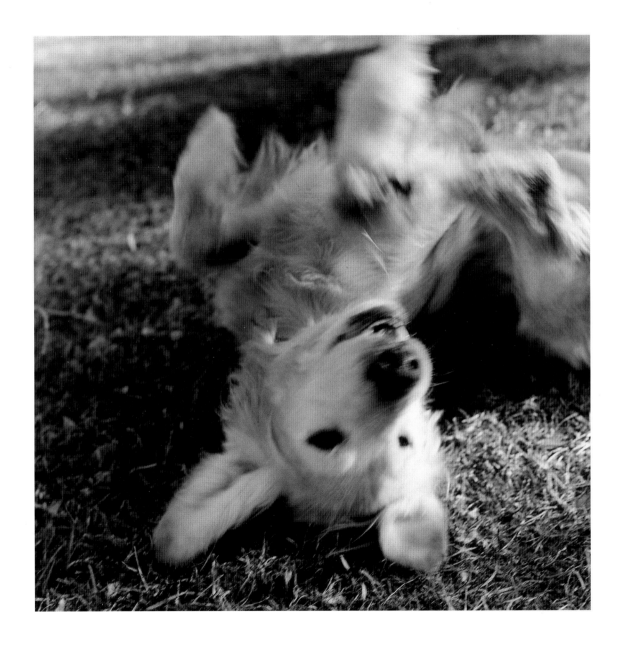

I got it! It's mine! I'm fully extended!

And partly in water, too — even more splendid!

And aren't I grateful you condescended

To throw it "once more." If you comprehended

The game you'd know it's only suspended,

Never over, it's *open-ended!*

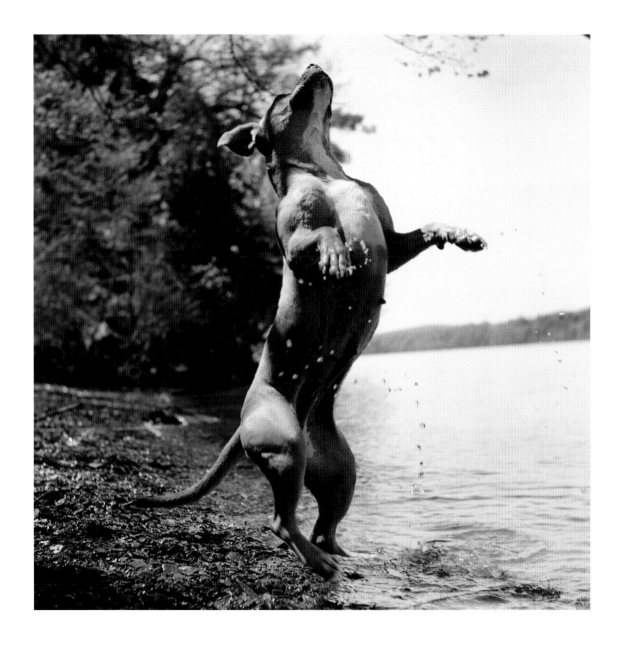

What does that mean, "expensive shoe"?
I ate it because it smelled like you.

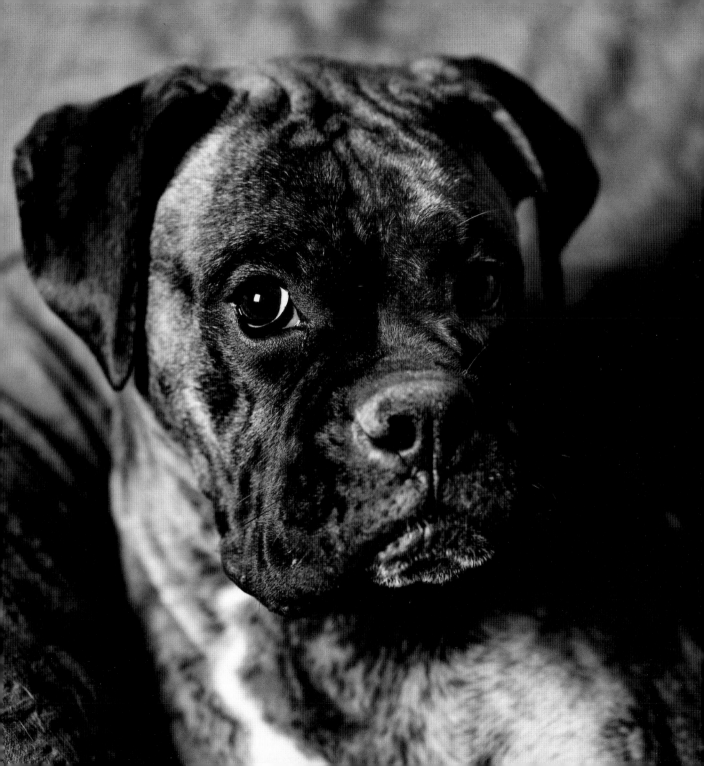

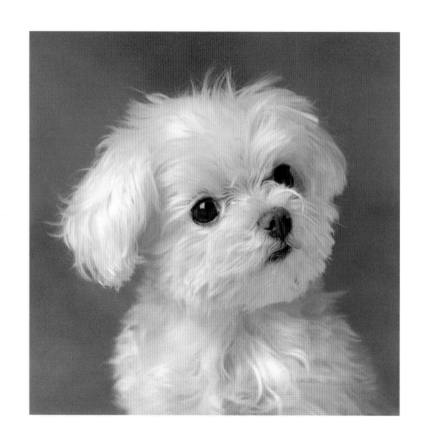

Why yes, I am real.

And what is your deal?

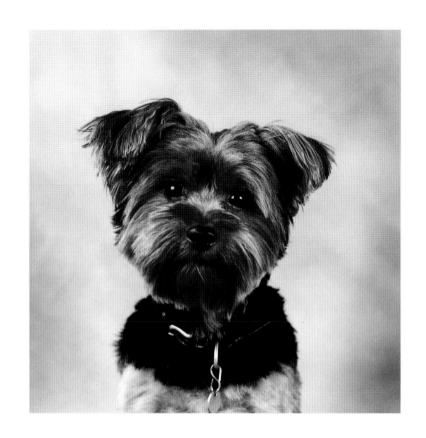

Aren't I precious? I guess so.

Everybody says so.

I'm smaller than the cat!

What's up with that?

They reach out to pet other dogs, not me.
They say,

       "*What kind* of dog is *he*?"
They say to other dogs, "Aren't *you* nice?'

       This has happened to me just twice.
       Both times blind men.
              Blind men know
       What I may lack the looks to show.

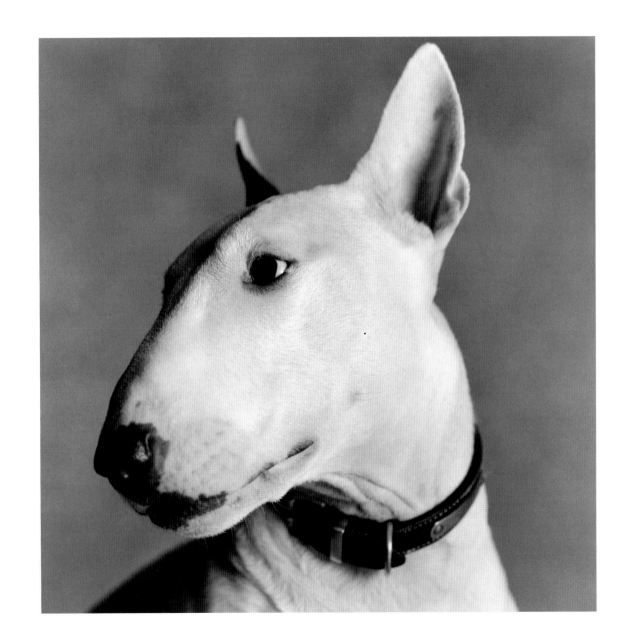

Hear that ocean crash and heave.

Nothing you can throw in it we can't retrieve.

Far as the nose of dog can reach,

We are the dogs of this here beach.

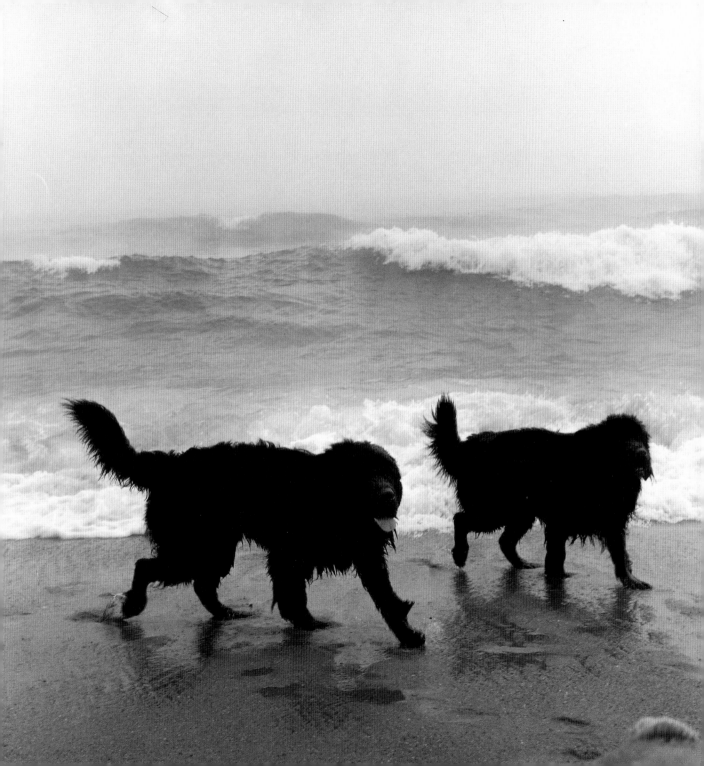

By the sea,
By the sea.

What's *this* I see?
By the beautiful sea.

I *bark* at the sea,
Bark, *bark* at the sea.

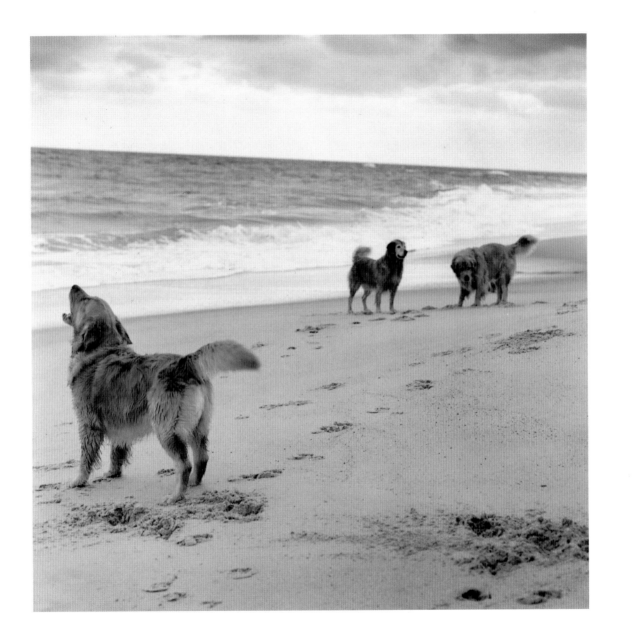

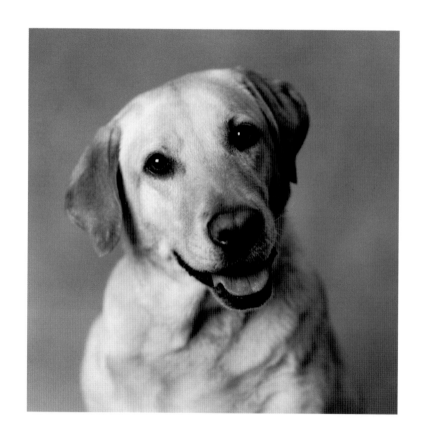

I'm a simple dog, really.

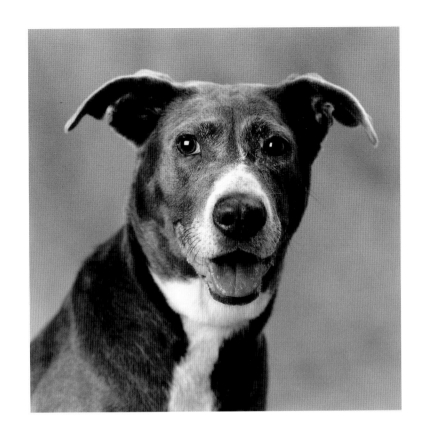

Me, too. Heh-heh.

The move came at a bad time for me.

That squirrel I buried in the leafwallow . . .

And now I'll never see

What was hiding in the loghollow.

They can't have known.

Here, there's just a small "lawn."

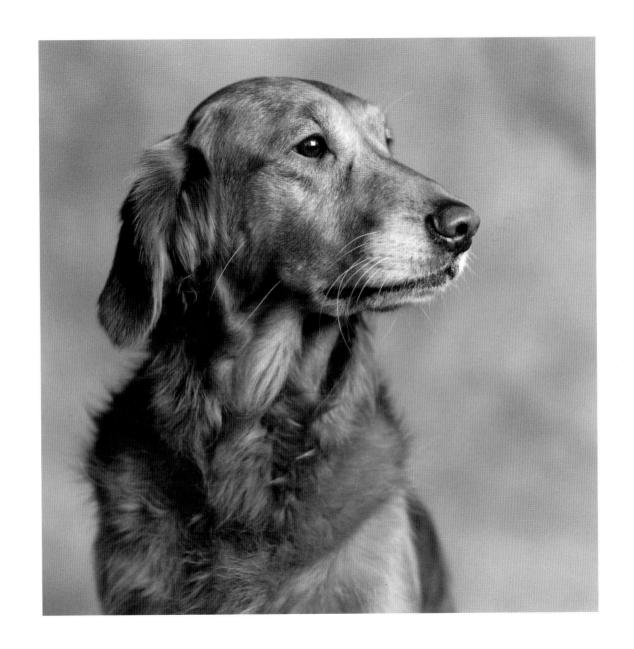

You say I am cute.

It doesn't compute.

What I am, is befuddled.

It's good to be cuddled,

But this getting

Petted for wetting

     One place on the floor

     And not another . . .

I can't help dribbling!

And where are those siblings

     I had before?

     And didn't I have a mother?

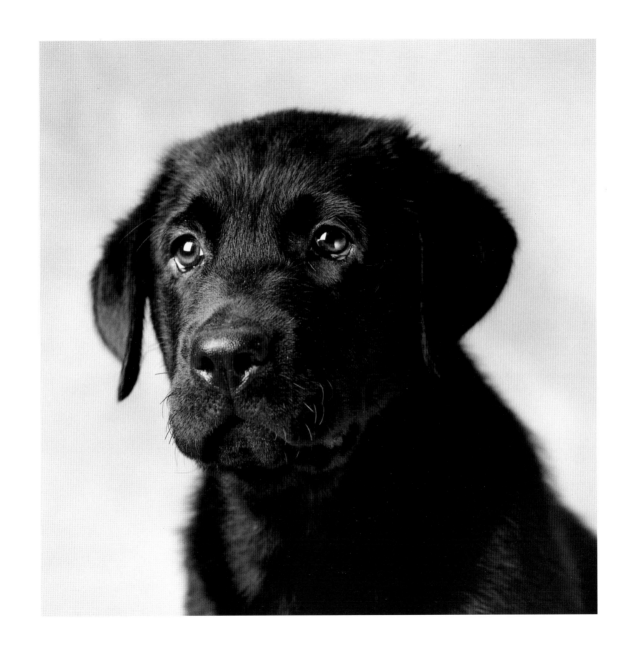

"Two dogs are better than one."

"As long as I'm the one."

"So why am I outrunning you?"

"You're running *from* me."

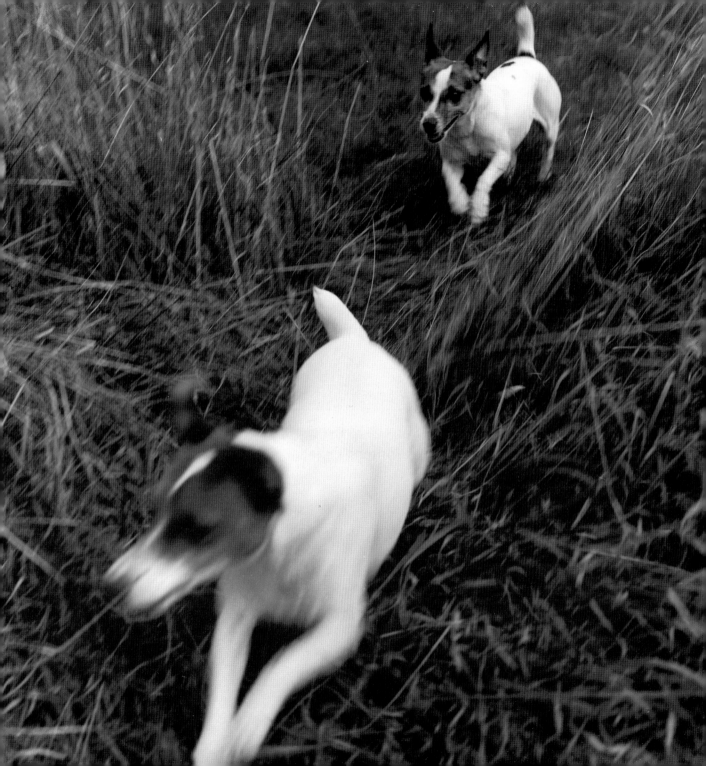

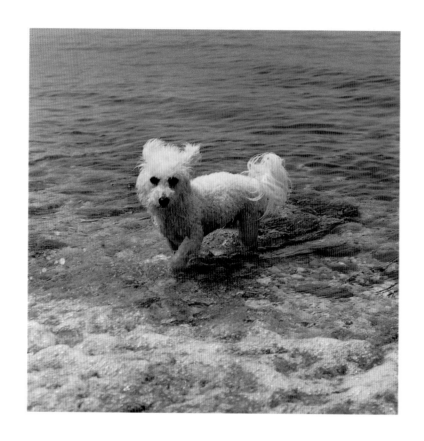

Oo, feels nice, though what it does
To my coat makes me feel rather naked.

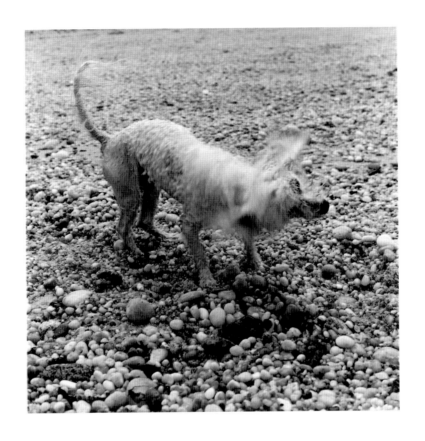

Well, it's *good* to cut the fuzz —
Then shake it, baby, shake it.

I don't quite get what you're saying . . .
Something about "obeying"?
Maybe I'm dumb.
Going out? Can I come?

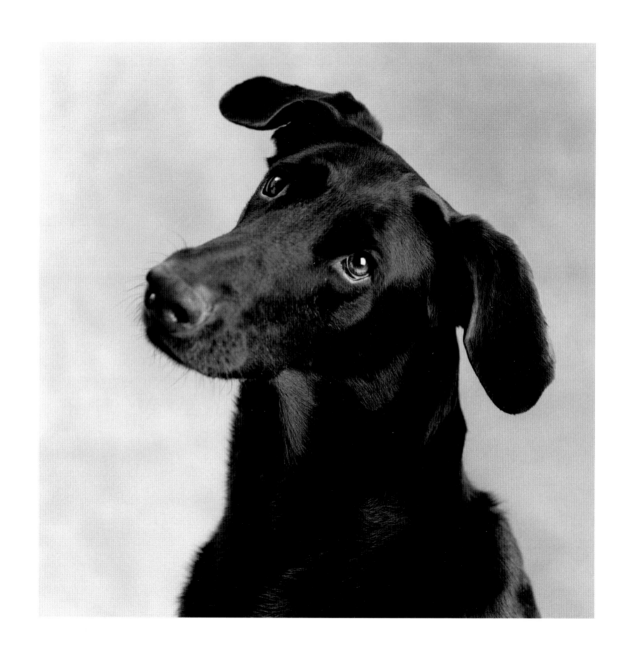

"Good dog"?
Oh, thanks so much,
Ms. Good Person.

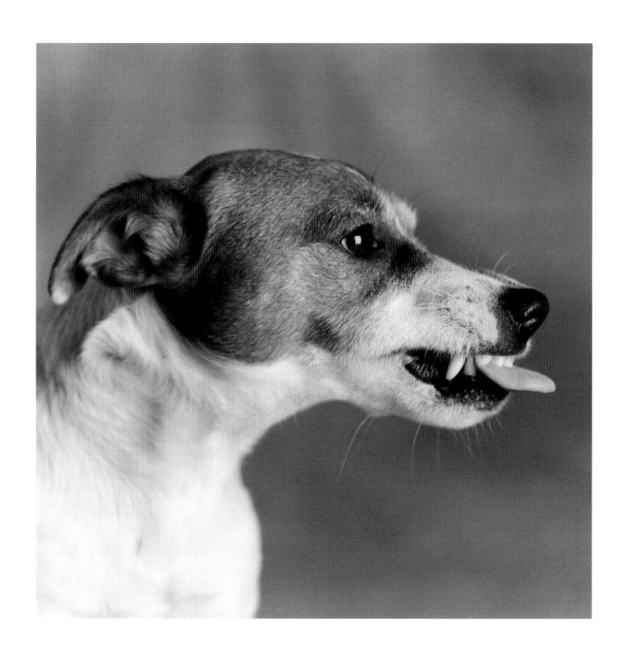

Whatever I did, I know I shouldn't.

If I knew what it was, I know I wouldn't.

All I know is to give you this look

Till you let me know I'm off the hook.

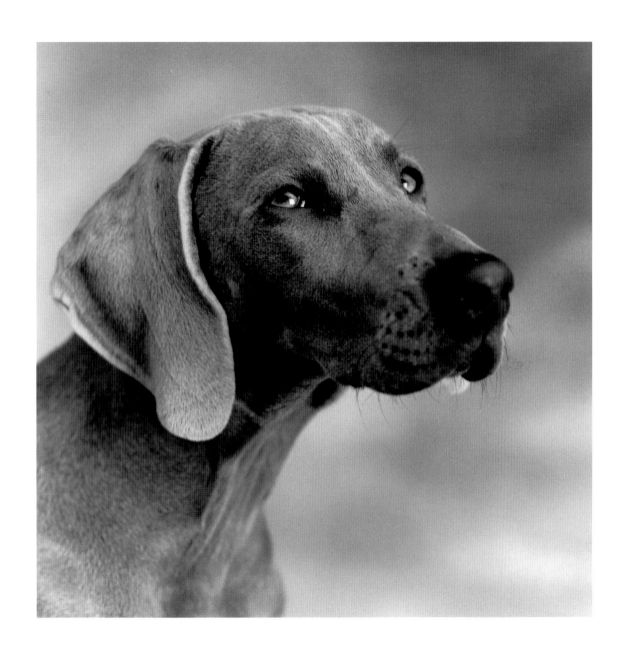

Clickity, clonkity — gosh,

The hounds lope onto the dock.

Clickity skritchity clonk,

Dockity rockity bonk —

Who's gonna tell 'em

They're out of their ele-

Ment? Clickity lopity *splosh*.

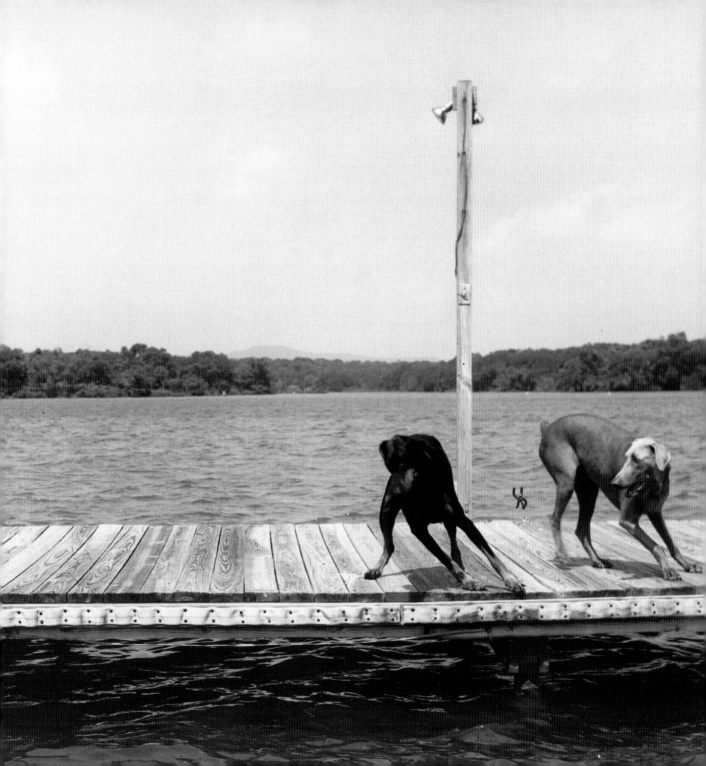

Can't you see what I'm trying to tell you?
If only you knew how much I smell you.

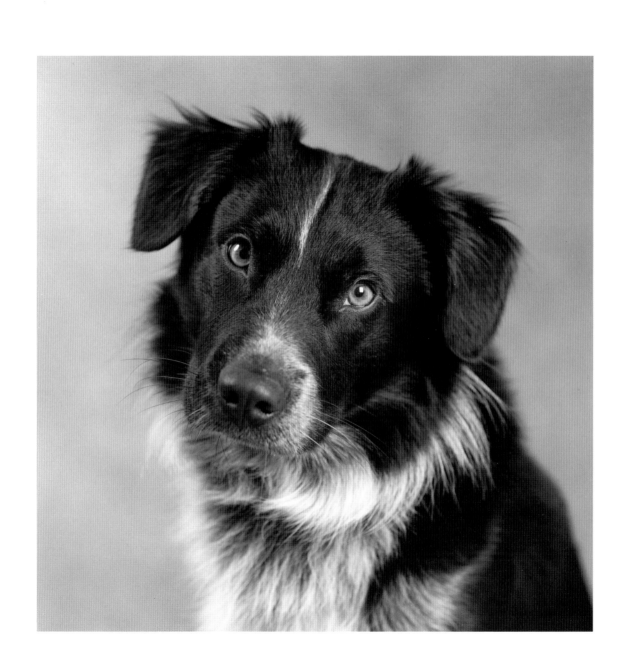

They keep me chained.
It's never explained.

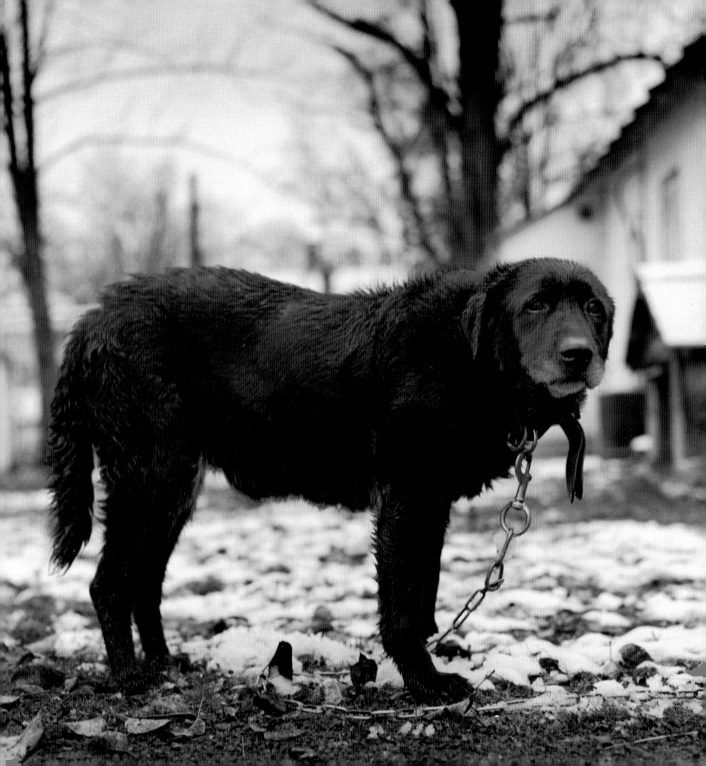

Got my belly on a cool spot,
Belly on a cool spot,
Tongue out in the air,
And anything that comes my way
I'll chase it everywhere.

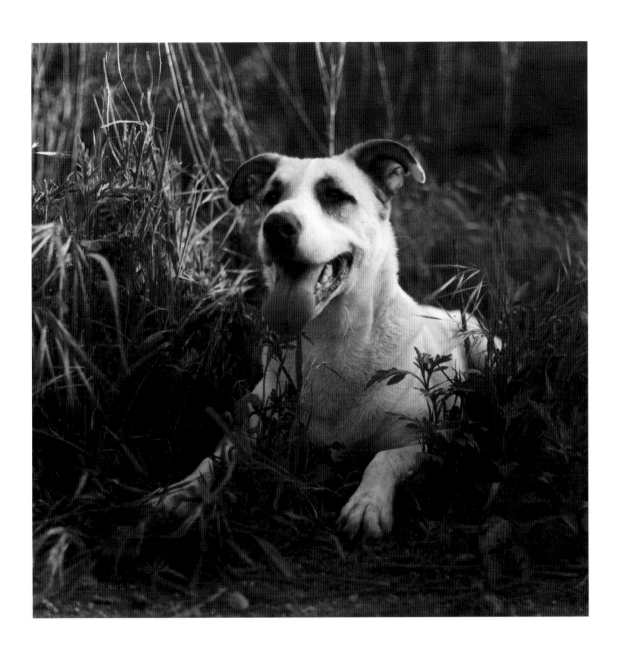

Oh, hey . . .

You say

    that I . . .

        "know"

            I "don't belong"

                on the couch?

                On the couch,

            for me, is wrong?

        Oh.

    But I . . .

Okay!

Okay!

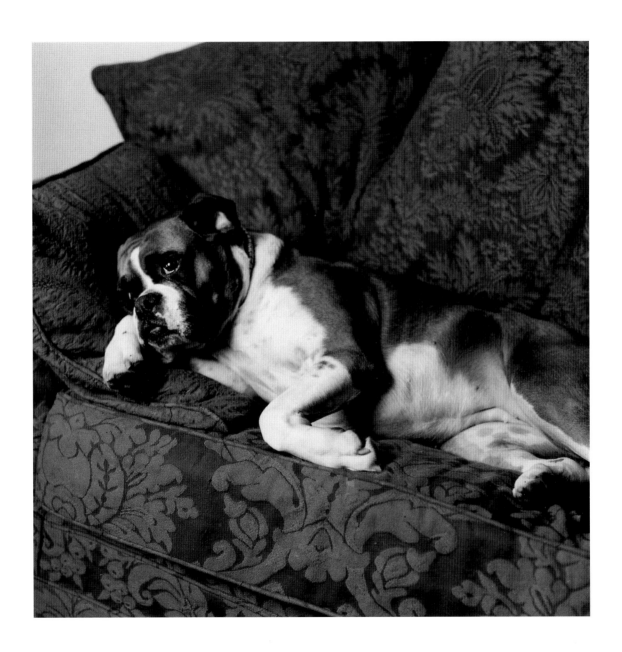

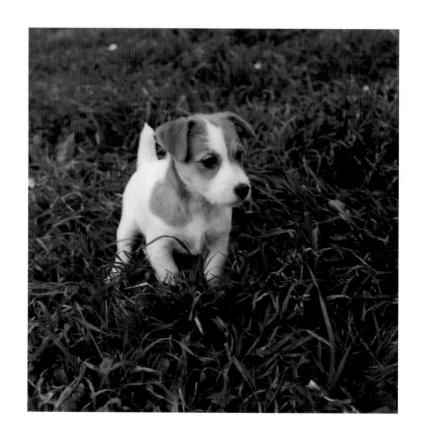

Don't call *me* your "little furball."

I'm on the trail of something terrible.

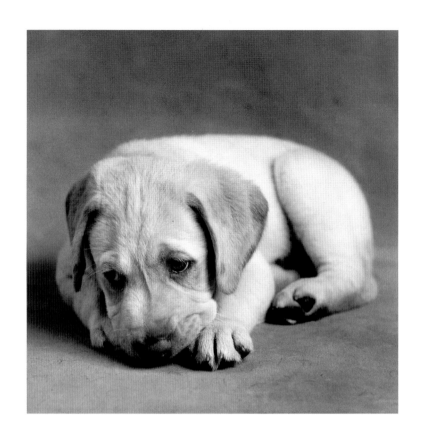

I was having such fun and then
I got tired.
Will I ever have fun again?

Huh? Get up? I'm up.

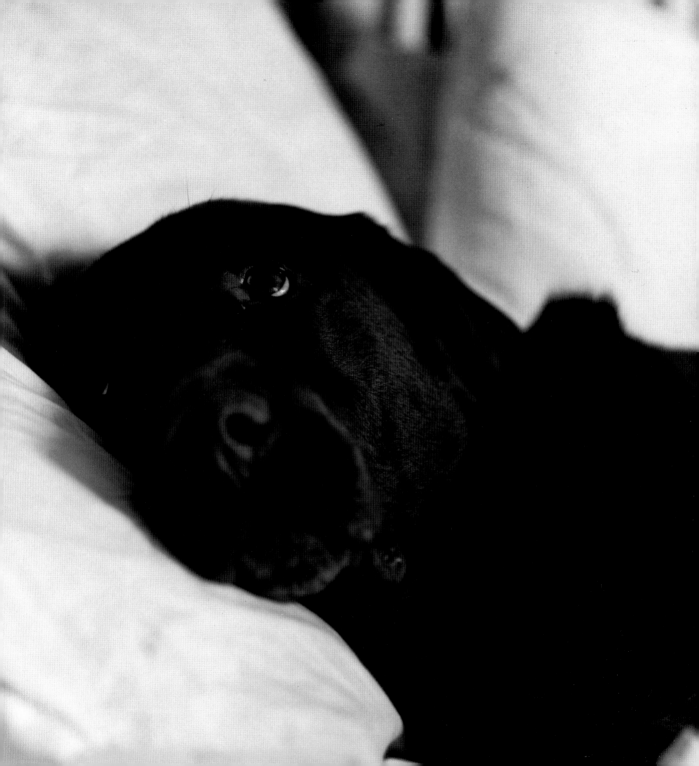

I had such dreams.

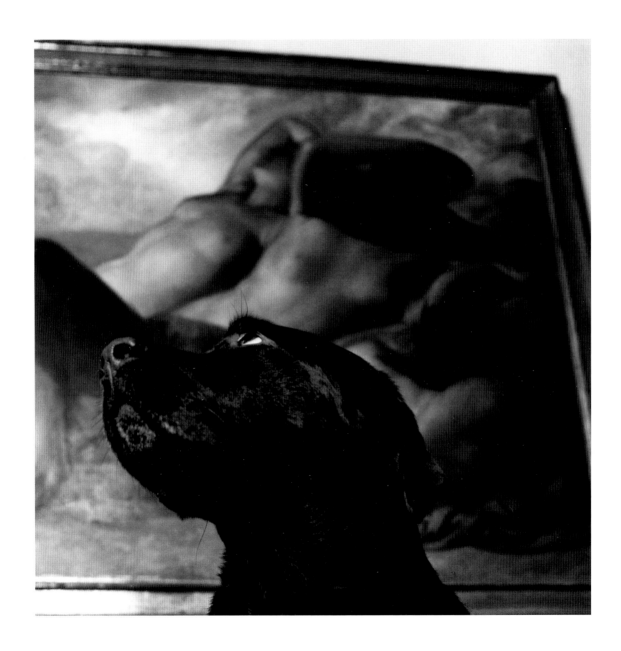

You said sit here, I sat here,
For which I feel no affinity.
Now, let's go out —
You want me to doubt
My own caninity?
This is a place for a cat, here.

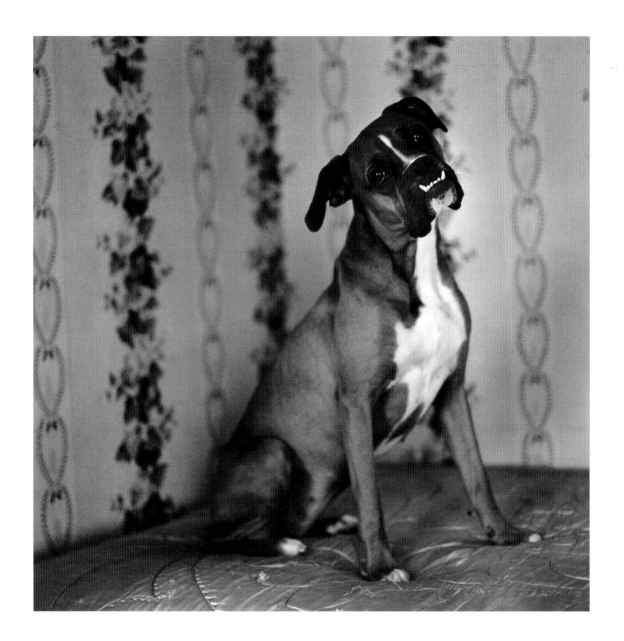

"Do you ever hear from somewhere way back deep — "

"The call of the wild? No. Let me sleep."

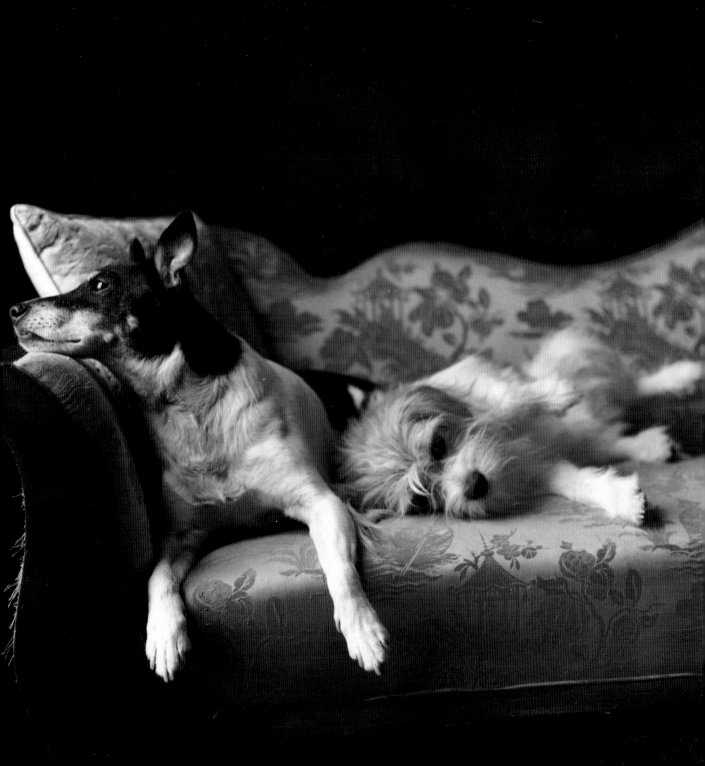

Surf is up,

       I'm leaning into the wind.

Surf is up,

       I'm leaning into the wind.

Throw that tennis ball, mama,

          I'll run get it again.

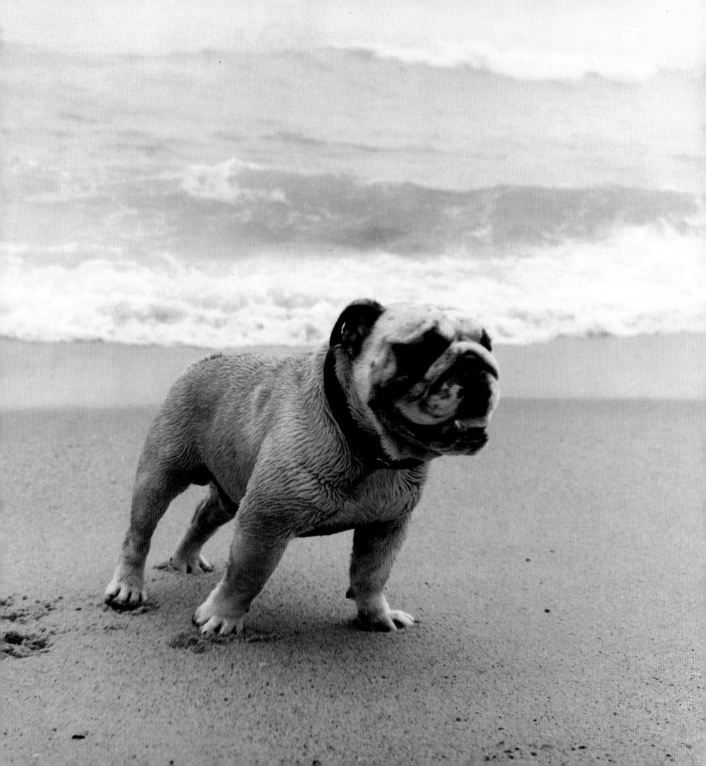

First Paperback Edition, 2003

ISBN 0-8212-2830-7

Library of Congress Control Number 97-77747

Front cover design by John Kane

Bulfinch Press is a division of AOL Time Warner Book Group

PRINTED IN ITALY